SYMBIOSIS

Poet

Barbara Guest

Artist

Laurie Reid

A version of this poem appeared in the Vancouver B.C. magazine *Raddle Moon*, edited by Susan Clark.

Publication of this book was made possible by a grant from the California Arts Council and generous donations by the Friends of the Collaboration Series. Special thanks to the following Friends: Penelope Cooper, Louise Gund, the LEF Foundation, Diane Middlebrook, Barclay and Sharon Simpson, Sandra J. Springs, and Earlene Taylor.

Series produced by Rena Rosenwasser.

Library of Congress Cataloging-in-Publication Data

First Edition

Guest, Barbara
Symbiosis / poet, Barbara Guest; artist, Laurie Reid--1st ed.
p. cm.
ISBN: 0-932716-52-0 (alk. paper) $17
ISBN: 0-932716-54-7 (alk. paper) (35 limited signed editions with an original drawing by the artist) $200
I. Reid, Laurie, 1964-II. Title.

PS3513.U44 S96 2000
811'.54—dc21

00-032746

Kelsey St. Press kelseyst.com
All orders to: Small Press Distribution
510.524.1668 orders@spdbooks.org

A writer and an artist working together establish a Symbiosis, as in Nature, where dissimilar organisms productively live together.

Hiss
the wool
fable,

close and away.

Hiss in turning wool,

and envied the circle
and volume,

working in layers.

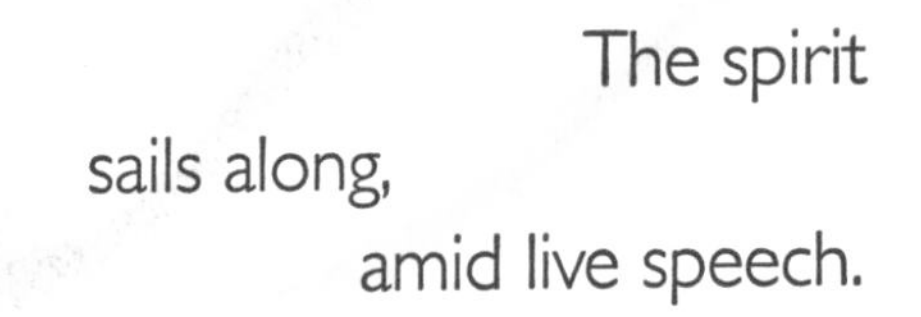

The spirit
sails along,
amid live speech.

"Ripening beyond sheer height," calls itself.

Is symbiosis aflame   stroked

each line   power wound up in volume,
when spoken to, fear in place of the woven,

often, it says, in place of the line.
Thinned down, staggering   looks up to the drawing;

bodies all the way up the hill.

Will it belong, or is symbiosis aflame each pine stroking,

symbiosis aflame,

each day autumn. Day awakens, no break in the thread.

Needing, needing, needing

over the surface perpendicular

is not something to chat about filled
by iridescence.

They talk about
loosened bones. Could be a shuttle

if it worked in direct light.

The thread loose

as any from the underworld,

more in iridescence, hidden.

A suggestion in mid air

dropped on the hid body, no nerve blinding nothing
attached,

no weight, no thing to litter,

free as unusual.

Plume of impatience the petal,

a clue to ensnare the undrawn,

O valley. O wine.

This is the point where the strophes meet,

one line interweaves with another,

room of liberal fountains,

a different speech and metabolism,

near an ancient site of accord

and priority.

In no climate whatsoever

noise traveling up the tower

bronze green in the tournament,

each player hit a wood ball.

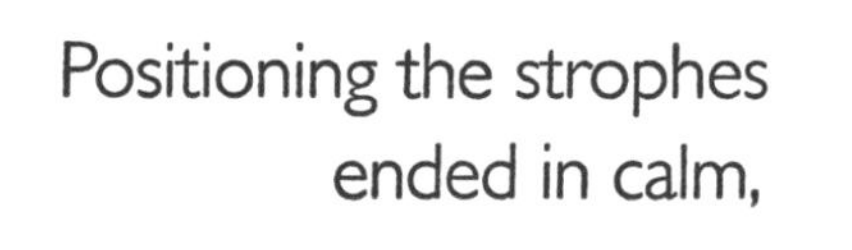

Positioning the strophes
ended in calm,

after the strophes are positioned.

Knitting or singing a song, hair let down

from the blue—ranging and tumbling the blue

magnolia nestled, the wild berry, also.

This is a strange way to tell a story being

where one does not wish, in the midst of a storm...

Gas lights and lost

the cares of thought, an oil lamp, Maupassant

put it there. He stands at the window.

She places her hands on her hair.

She looks at a Poem-Painting

"The walks of Saint Cloud

are open,

the eyes of the fish

are closed.

Remarkable basins,

you give me ten years."

The difficult! the difficult!

loosen the ropes that entangle it,

tear them down from the mast!

The schooner off its route,

adios to the bird of prey,

flies in another direction, the nineteenth

century

wears a plaid cap.

Say *adios* when you see

the figure from the mainland crossing on tiles.

And they have no intention to avoid

the gaze of symbiosis,
or the century,

pasting and printing in the same room

—sharing
the furry moment draped over their head,

light from the transom.

A sign of being gentle,

the scene is more mature.

She is not so silly

as they thought in her mantle,

coming from outside

studying to be someone else,

why not? And write her own script,

write it then she did

first learn about pretense   the make-up and lounge dress,

authority and the syllabus.

A tendency to respond (lacquer) near the driveway, she was

thought not pliable or overtly sensitive. She is more fluid,

she is outside.

Coming from outside, fluid orange.

Rhythm

and festivity.

A sign of being gentle, plain orange.

She can read the image in the overlapping

even from outside,

those parts that overlap,

lip and facial movement,

color of the image as it changes—

pushed her leg through the rippling

image changes.

Symbiosis is a limited edition of
one thousand five hundred copies;
thirty-five are numbered and signed
and include an original
drawing by the artist.
Text printed on letterpress
by Peter Koch Printers.
Drawings produced by
West Coast Print Center.
Mohawk Superfine Eggshell text.
Proterra Antique Stucco cover.
Text is set in Gill Sans.
Book design by Robert Rosenwasser.

Kelsey St. Press 2000